THE GENTLE BROTHER

Some further books of White Eagle's Teaching:

GOLDEN HARVEST
HEAL THYSELF
MORNING LIGHT
PATH OF THE SOUL
THE QUIET MIND
SPIRITUAL UNFOLDMENT I
SPIRITUAL UNFOLDMENT II
SUNRISE
WISDOM FROM WHITE EAGLE

THE GENTLE
BROTHER

WHITE EAGLE

THE WHITE EAGLE PUBLISHING TRUST
NEW LANDS · LISS · HAMPSHIRE

First Edition: November 1968

Reprinted: November 1974

© *Copyright, The White Eagle Publishing Trust, 1968*

ISBN 0 85487 002 4

PRINTED IN GREAT BRITAIN BY
FLETCHER AND SON LTD, NORWICH

CONTENTS

FOREWORD   7

I   BE OF GOOD HEART   9

II   THE PASSWORD   19

III   YOU ARE IN GOD, AND GOD IS
PERFECT   29

IV   SEEK FIRST THE KINGDOM   40

V   BE STILL   51

VI   THINK, SPEAK AND ACT IN THE
LIGHT   58

White Eagle speaks through the instrumentality of Grace Cooke

Foreword

This book consists of short extracts from White Eagle's talks to Brothers of his Lodge, specially chosen to guide and help the aspirant in his daily life. These 'Gentle Brother' extracts have long been the most loved feature of the magazine, STELLA POLARIS, and many friends have asked if they could be collected and published in a small book suitable for the pocket or handbag or as a bedtime book.

White Eagle has the art of putting his finger right on the spot, as it were, of one's particular problem, and giving a wise, practical and helpful answer. For years he has been a friend to many people, and those who know his voice will be reminded of his gentle form of expression, and the voice of authority with which he speaks. The basis of his wisdom will be found in the scriptures of the world, and especially in the four gospels of Christianity.

So here is White Eagle's book, with his love and blessing.

GRACE COOKE

I

Be of Good Heart

We would speak to each one individually if it were possible. We know more than you realise about your own personal sorrows, responsibilities and anxieties. We see you in your individual little clouds. We see that you are anxious for a friend or family; maybe you are lonely and long for greater realisation and completion of love in your own hearts and lives. Or perhaps you feel frustrated and unable to do the spiritual work of which you feel capable. These thoughts and feelings appear as little and sometimes as big clouds about you.

We know through our own past experience and from what we can see in you and on the path before you, that if, in imagination, you will place both your hands in those of your divine Parents, the Father–Mother God, the Father holding one hand, the Mother holding the other, so that the triangle between you and your divine Parents is complete, then Light will shine on your life, your fears will dissolve, and you will discover later on that your cloud has a silver lining. You will find completion, happiness, service.

But remember God does not hurry. We, His children, must accept God's own pace. We must be patient. When we become impatient and reject an opportunity, or run off to find another amusement or a fresh interest, we waste so much time, for the same procedure will have to be repeated, right up to the very point where the lesson of patience and calmness of spirit has to be mastered.

But if we 'keep on keeping on' thankfully and trustfully along the appointed path, we shall be blessed with achievement, with completion, with a happiness such as the world cannot give, and a peace such as the world cannot take away.

2

While we are here with you on earth we participate in your life, your thoughts, your sorrows, but we do not take them with us when we rise into the spirit realms; instead we bring happiness and love down to you.

We want you to come up as often as you can into this sphere of harmony and truth, so that you become immersed in it—just as a sponge, immersed, becomes full of water. You will become full of the light and harmony of those higher spheres, and then the darkness will have no power over you.

Many saints have known a supreme happiness even while living in comparative poverty. Nothing in the material world is so important as the love of God in your heart. When you leave the body you will leave behind all physical things. Then, if your heart is full of love and peace you will be in heaven, but if your heart is full of enmity, discontent and unhappiness you will not be in heaven. This is why the Master declares that nothing is so important as the love of Christ in your heart. Problems of the material world will all pass away, they will disappear, they are unimportant. Concentrate on this inner light, tranquillity, joy of the spirit, and you have everything.

3

The sage says: the wise grieve neither for the living nor for those who have passed into the spirit world. The wise know that there is no death. The wise know that there is an all-loving Father–Mother God Who watches over the children on earth and Who sends guardian angels to care for them.

One of the most difficult lessons that has to be mastered is that of surrender to your all-wise and loving Parents. There is so much that you cannot understand in human relationship. Very often you have to endure what seems to be injustice, but it is only a question of being patient. Compensations come into the human life to balance what appears to be injustice. You must take the long view, and those in the spirit world who can see further than you, will always tell you that all crooked places will be made straight. So have patience; take the long view; give your confidence to the Great White Spirit. All injustice will be righted.

Be of good heart, in time every one of you will have cause to say, 'God is wonderful in His method of working out karmic law.'

The magical power of the Christ spirit is active in the world, working slowly and silently behind the scenes to perfect human life. We ask you to remain steadfast in your conviction that this magical power can and will raise all men. If you do this, you will be working in harmony and in co-operation with God's law.

You are enfolded in the love of all the White Brethren, joyous, thankful and secure.

All is well. There is nothing to fear. Take up your duties. Keep on keeping on quietly day by day filled with this joyous assurance, and walk life's pathway hand in hand and heart to heart with these radiant ones and with your brethren who work with you.

God will not leave you. Give your trust, that is all. The light within you, the inner voice, will tell you truly your duty; then do that duty, and look into the face of your Master without fear.

4

The only path for man is the way of confidence in God, in His perfect Wisdom. If you place your confidence in God, you are prepared to accept life as it is, *knowing* that it cannot be other than good; it is given to you in love, and all the circumstances of your life must be combining to bring good, to bring growth, to bring light and progress.

To trust God means that you are absolutely at peace. You see life as a process of growth, and what appears so ugly and distressing you see as a condition which will ultimately bring beauty and perfection in the life of man.

If you have confidence in God you will remain untouched by anything the world can do. You will no longer be confused and troubled, once you have found confidence in God.

Nothing is real except the love and wisdom of God. You say, 'But the problem of suffering is very real to those who are passing through it!' But we answer, the one who is suffering can find relief from that suffering through complete surrender to the goodness and love of God. Suffering comes because the individual is unaware of the presence of God; he is separate, alienated from the love of God.

The problem of suffering cannot be understood while the pupil is bound by the limitations of the physical and material life. As soon as he can free himself from these limitations, even though still living in the physical body, he will understand, and see suffering in its true perspective. But this necessitates a continual aspiration to God-realisation. There must be a determination to be on God's side, a continual application and attention by the pupil always to walk God's way. Live with the thought that God is good.

Try to realise that Christ's kingdom is *in you*; and also that you live in it, in Christ's kingdom of the Star. If you can realise this perfect life within, in time it must manifest in your life, in your surroundings. This is the natural law . . . as above, so below; as below, so above.

5

With God all things are possible, but the child of God must be in complete at-one-ment with the Father. There must be no doubt, no fear, but simple surrender to the Great White Spirit. This is the way that so-called miracles are performed, but the trouble is that the contact between man and God is not sustained. You know these things in your *mind*, you may have read them in the scriptures, but you do not know them with your heart. To do so means patient application and humble surrender. Put into practice this divine law. All brethren of the Great White Light learn to realise their at-one-ment with the Father.

Never doubt, for doubt brings down your temple. Never doubt the Brotherhood. Never doubt God's power or God's laws. The flesh itself may be weak, but as the spirit waxes strong the body is filled with light, and is recharged with divine energy.

May you all experience a full realisation of the words of the Master, who said: 'The Father is in me, and I in him.' Cultivate the habit of drawing upon the divine, eternal Presence, and your being will be flooded with light. You will learn as you advance on the spiritual path how the power of God in you can be used to re-create and reform all the conditions of your life. Within man lies the power to change the very atoms of his body, for the physical atoms are the spiritual atoms. These tiny sparks of light are the power behind all visible form. These atoms can be changed by the command of God. The whole of life is under the direction and command of the Great White Light.

The purpose of incarnation is for you to bring through into daily life the radiance of your spiritual life. We know your difficulties; we know how the physical body holds you fast in its grip; and through it you suffer fears and pains, disorders of mind and spirit. In the words of Jesus, we say, 'Rise! take up your bed (the material life), and walk.' Walk the path of light. Seek the true Source of your being, and you will triumph over the darkness of physical matter.

6

Why do you fear for your daily needs? He who knows not of God's love fears for his life, but not a Son of Light. If you allow yourself to be driven like cattle, and become full of fear and anxiety, being a dis-eased soul you are unable to minister to the needs of your fellows. The only way to bring peace on earth is for each individual soul to become a centre of peace. This is the secret of mastership and dominion over material life.

Therefore, link yourself daily to the Prince of Peace. Would you enter His presence in a state of turmoil and fret? Indeed, you could not get near Him. If you would approach Him, you must first become at peace within yourself. You must approach Him tranquilly, with humility and love.

He says, 'No man can serve two masters . . . ye cannot serve God and Mammon.' Mammon does not necessarily mean worldly possessions; it means the worldly mind, pride of intellect, mental arrogance; a man who worships Mammon trusts in his own power, thinking of himself as great. The wise man knows that God alone is great.

Follow God or good; take the gentle way, offer the other cheek, be guided by your intuition, and love; and you will have chosen the better path, the path of God. Mental arrogance and pride bow in service to Mammon. They corrupt and bear the seeds of future sorrow.

Fear is a weakness of the lower mind. The lower mind suggests limitation and failure; it suggests failure of the spiritual powers to save the world. Do not be guilty of this negative thinking. Know that God is all-love, all-wisdom. His power is infinite. God cannot fail. Man may bring unnecessary suffering upon himself, but God ever works, like the great physician, to heal mankind's wounds. Do not be tempted to look on the negative side. What you do not understand, leave aside; but never fail to trust God's love.

And now, the peace of the eternal stillness, the tranquillity of spirit abide with you in all your ways.

II

The Password

We are aware of your individual problems. We know the heart of each one of you, and the struggles and the difficulties you have to face. The stones that cut your feet as you tread the path of life have first cut ours. When you have set your feet on the spiritual path you will receive indescribable happiness and joy, but there will also be times when you will experience sorrow, hurt, disappointment. This is because the two aspects in your nature, the higher and the lower, come into conflict. Before you had set your feet on that path, life was perhaps not so complicated, you did not feel the responsibility or the strong urge of the inner light, or what some people call conscience. But once you have realised the truth of your being, and your higher self is awakened, the issue must be faced. For a time you are happy; and then human problems arise, and the desire nature asserts itself and seeks to justify its actions. There is conflict—you are no longer at peace.

Do not be disheartened by these experiences for they are healthy. You are on the way to find deeper joy and happiness which no pleasures of the senses can ever give you, and the struggle is worth while. Having set your feet upon the Path, then look towards God, praying for His strength and help in overcoming the niggling temptations of the lower self—not only of the body, but of the mind, which tempts you to be arrogant, proud and resentful. These temptations must be faced and overcome.

In simplicity then, beloved brethren, let us turn to the figure of our Elder Brother, the beautiful character and presence of Jesus the Christ. People will tell you that this is an ideal impossible of realisation on earth. This is not true, for in the course of your spiritual evolution you will have at some time to show through a physical body and earthly personality all the characteristics of the Son of God. Let it therefore be your constant aspiration now, to manifest the Christ light in every thought, word and action.

2

One of the most difficult lessons to learn is that of patience. Impatience holds back many a soul who is on the spiritual path. And in the inner mystery schools of the past, the candidate was always taught the inadvisability of rushing forward too quickly, because by being too eager he might be blinded. Therefore man must work patiently with his chisel and gavel upon the rough ashlar of his being, which he can only hope to perfect with long and patient work.

Learn patience, and you will enter into that peace which brings power.

The second quality we would speak of is love. Perhaps you think we should have put love first? But patience is necessary in order to learn love. When we speak of love, we do not mean sentiment or emotion. Love is of the spirit, and by it you recognise the spirit in your brother man. Love refrains from judgement, never attributes motives to another, for God alone knows the heart of your brother. It is so easy to misjudge. Refrain always. If you do not understand, know that the time will come when you *will* understand the reason for certain things happening.

Without love, power is destructive and self-consuming. The fires of power, longing for power, consume the soul; the warmth of love gives life. It is not enough to say, 'I love'; love must be your innermost and spontaneous response towards every soul you encounter. You must know that your brother is striving towards the Light, even as you are.

Try to translate this ideal into daily life, and never fail to be loving in your intercourse with your brother man.

3

On the spiritual path are many seeming contradictions. You will be told to be very careful and to think before you speak or act. Later on the path you will be told you must learn to act spontaneously, to be quick and wise on the spur of the moment. You are at present at the stage where you must learn to be very guarded, very careful in speech. The wise man learns so much through silence. How wise is he who has learnt to discriminate between what to say, and what to leave unsaid! Wise also is he who can listen to the spoken word and understand the language of the spirit behind. You know the story of the wise old owl who sat on a tree, and looked and listened? Learn to be wise, to be silent, and to listen.

You want to listen to the spirit world, to listen to the words of love spoken by your beloved in the beyond, by your guide, your teacher, and later by your master? Learn then to listen first to people on the earth, to give your whole attention to the one who is speaking to you; listen also to the sounds of the birds and animals, the song of the wind in the trees, of the falling raindrops and the rushing river. This is how the Red Indians were trained from childhood; and because they were so trained, they were able to hear not only physical sounds, but sounds *behind* those of earth, the sounds of the unseen world. They could distinguish the voices of their spirit guides and teachers; they could also hear the nature spirits. It is difficult for you in these noisy cities to hear anything of these, yet you must train yourself to listen.

4

It is a human and natural instinct to be righteously indignant when you see injustice. In the early stages of the development of love in your heart you will naturally want to protect the weaker; to right wrongs. This is understandable, but let us pause, my brethren, and consider the words in your Christian Bible: 'Resist not evil . . . but overcome evil with good.'

This does not mean that you should take no notice of evil, but that you should so fill your heart and life and environment with good, with love, with light, that evil is absorbed by the light.

The right way to remove darkness is to bring the light to shine upon it. The way to remove evil is for every soul who has seen the light to manifest light in his own life and to gently endeavour to pass on the truth he has received. If there were sufficient brethren in the world who could unite in groups and work together to project the light into the world there would be no need for protestation—the light would enter and permeate the hearts of all men, and in place of evil or darkness there would come goodness and light. This is the true way to combat evil.

Individually, if you find yourself rubbing against rough corners, either your own or other people's, try to smooth those corners by sending out love and the good thought of the white brother. Never mind about injustice, a stumbling block to so many. Many have said to me, 'Oh, White Eagle, it is the *injustice* that I cannot stand, it seems so unjust.' My dears, God is justice and you can be quite, quite certain that God will work out His justice to the very last degree. But *you* cannot enforce God's justice, this is impossible. You can, however, escape the suffering which the seeming injustice inflicts on you if you, as a white brother obey the law and follow the light. The one who inflicts the injustice can safely be left to the loving wisdom of God; and if you know God, you will know that absolute justice will be done.

We assure you, with all the love that is in our hearts for you, that the only way is the way of love. Let little things go; put them in their right perspective. Little things can become like mountains, but they can be very easily disposed of if you disregard them and train yourself to regard only the big things, the important things. Give way on little things that do not matter, but on matters of principle stand firm as a rock.

5

Spiritual law ordains that every man must pay and be paid for every service rendered. In the ancient schools of mysticism, in the schools of the Brotherhood, there was a saying that the brother must go to the temple to receive just payment for his work. This is another way of describing the law of cause and effect.

You need harbour no regrets, nor worry, 'should I have done this, or did I make a mistake?' The only real mistake you can make is when you do not react in the right way to the demand for payment which the law of karma brings. Therefore do not resent the things which you sometimes feel are very unjust. Do not grumble about your conditions, or about people who appear to have treated you badly, or who do not do as you think they should. Remember that all mankind is under the exact law of karma. As you on occasion have treated others, either in the past or even in the present, so you yourself will be treated in exactly the same way, not necessarily by the same person, but in the same coin. Whatever you have given you will receive, whether it is good or bad. You cannot escape this just law of karma. All that you give in service, in love; all that you give, even in material gifts, will be repaid in due time.

Never regret, dear ones, the episodes in your life that you feel have been unjust. Never wonder if a certain course of action was unwise. You learnt a lesson from it, or you should have done. This is the important point, that you are all on earth to *learn*, and you can only learn by experience. You need never doubt that eventually you will reap a golden harvest. Although the payment exacted at a particular time may seem to you unduly hard, nevertheless if you can accept that lesson in the right spirit it will do something to your own spirit; it will move you a step or many steps nearer to your ultimate happiness, your ultimate perfection. 'Eye hath not seen nor ear heard, neither hath entered into the heart of man the things which God hath prepared for them that love him.'

6

Always think in terms of the eternal Light. When things are not easy in your life, resign all in humility to the Light. As man attunes himself to the Light, so all good will come in him and in his life. Thus is he freed for ever from the limitations of physical matter.

In the heights, in the mountain tops there lives tranquillity and peace which is the power, the wisdom and the love behind all human life; and in the depths of your heart lies the same tranquillity which is the power, the wisdom and the love of your life. Do not forget to turn to that inner light for your succour and guidance. In that inner light you may meet the Brethren who work behind the scenes of the material life to send forth the light of the Star to suffering humanity. They—the Brethren—never doubt, they never look on the dark side; for they are

Brethren, and they live in the Light and work with the Light—they *are* the Light. Follow their example and teaching. Do not allow yourselves to think, still less to utter words of fear, doubt, or failure. Think, speak, and act in the Light, with the Light, confident that the new world will be built according to the plan of the Great White Brotherhood so long as the builders or masons are true.

Every White Brother knows that all is working for good, and that the Light absorbs the darkness everywhere.

III

You Are in God, and God is Perfect

The Brotherhood of the White Light is closely concerned with man's evolution, happiness, and well-being. We have passed through many incarnations and have the means of recalling these human experiences when necessary. Therefore we can feel with you; we can understand your frustrations, your limitations, and your anxieties and fears. We can understand bodily pain and spiritual suffering. We are part of you; we are one of you; we are with all of you.

But we love you; therefore we do not remove your problems and difficulties, for this would be neither kind nor good for you. We can only stand by your side and give you strength and love while you slowly learn by trial and error. As a result of your dealing with these difficulties, if you are on the path of light and are open to the message the spirit brings, you will receive into your souls joy which would be lost if we were to remove your problems and difficulties. Each time you see and follow the right way, each time you are able to touch the secret inner life, the light expands in your heart and soul, and life takes on a new appearance; you see with eyes both spiritual and physical a lovelier vista, a more radiant beauty than you have seen before, and your heart sings.

2

Always allow your intuition and your heart to take precedence over the earthly mind. Let your spiritual mind rule your lower mind; let it rule your life and all the happenings in your life. This does not mean that you must live 'out of this world', not at all. If you think with the mind in your heart, you are continually with God Who has the power to order your life perfectly. Also if you will open your heart as a little child and ask, you will receive the wisdom you seek. But do not ask in the wrong way. The right way is to have faith in God and know that God, Who is all love and wisdom, will satisfy your deepest need.

The way to pray is to put yourself into complete attunement with this cosmic spirit of love. Be in it, live in it, think of it, not of yourself and your earthly mind. Of yourselves you are nothing; you have no lasting power, no lasting wisdom or love. But when you dwell in the centre of the Star, or of that heavenly Light, you become great, because you are then consciously with God and God is with you; and all things must work together for good when you are with good or with God.

3

Do not look behind you. Do not regret mistakes, but be thankful for every experience, however painful, which has helped you to gain a clearer understanding.

Focus your thoughts and your vision above the material plane. We have to use these words, but at the same time we fully understand that spirit and matter are one. But *you* do not understand this yet. Man has to live his life in *full consciousness* of spirit. Man is spirit living in form, and that form is constituted out of spirit. Therefore the external life of man is a manifestation of the degree of spirit in him, or what he permits to manifest through his life and through his physical body of that pure and perfect life and light of the Creator.

We hope that you will meditate on our

words because all your future work and individual and collective happiness is based on this
fundamental truth. When you can, by train-
ing, put aside lesser things in order to enter
into the greater things of the spirit, you will
then find the true help and guidance you need.
Do not become so immersed in material details
that you cut yourself off from your source of
supply.

Time spent in good thought is never wasted.

Each time you resist the temptation to
resort to the lower mind and the thoughts of the
material world, and respond instead to the light
from your higher self, you are growing stronger
in spirit; and more, you are increasing the
power of the Light on earth.

4

We never fail to answer you when you call to us
on the inner planes, but you do not always hear
us. You need greater faith and trust, you need
to disentangle yourselves from the doubts and
fears of earth life. You *want* to believe, but you
are not always strong enough. You are like
young plants rooted in the dark earth, and
struggling to send up green shoots. This growth
is the purpose of everyday life, but it does

require strong and sustained effort from the spirit within you.

Do not be dismayed by the darkness that you witness in humanity, but cultivate compassion for life—not a superiority but a sweet, gentle compassion. It is difficult, we know, but you must keep on practising. Manifest the higher life in your own being. Every day, before you start your daily work, practise this, even if only for five minutes. Stop your outer activity and quietly ask God for His grace and love. Send your thoughts to those in spirit, both human and angelic, who watch and help you. Let this spiritual life become alive for you, so that it is always with you. Practise the presence of God even if only for five minutes in the morning and a few minutes before sleep; and do not, we beg you, be overwhelmed by the ignorance and darkness around you. It does no good to dwell on darkness. Look up to the Light and pray to become greater channels for the Light. Refuse to listen to the lower mind when it tempts you to give way to despondency. God is all goodness, love, and wisdom, and all things work together for good for the man who loves God. Do not despair; do not dwell on the negative side of any situation, for you will do no good by this. Always put into operation the forces of construction. *Believe* that good will come and the best is coming, and it will.

We do not speak in loud language of the things of the spirit; it is better not to shout from the hilltops and so we just keep quietly on, you with us, and we with you. Your hearts are full of love and we are grateful to you for every thought of yours which is of God. We cannot tell you how much you achieve by your kind and good thought.

5

It is important that you develop strength and poise. You must become dispassionate, turning your thoughts outward towards the well-being of men, instead of inwardly brooding over your own little hurts, faults, and failings. Many people waste too much time in introspection; they wonder if this or that is right, if this or that is wrong—so eager and anxious are they to progress. But this is a weakness which must be overcome. A few mistakes do not matter. It is what you are *thinking*, what you contribute in love, compassion, and great-heartedness to humanity that is important.

You love the spirit world and your spirit friends; but you would be even happier if you realised how happy you make them when you *think aright*; not only about your own troubles and little difficulties on the path, but towards other people. We know that some will find this difficult, but in time it will become spontaneous and part of your lives.

May the Light within your heart grow brighter as the years advance. May it be to you a sacred trust, that you never let your light grow dim.

6

You may wonder why sometimes you find it practically impossible to realise or even feel the presence of spiritual beings; and at others you feel so sure of their presence.

Why is it that sometimes you feel so blank and heavy, and at other times you feel as if you are on a mountain top, with clean bright air about you? In this lightened state you can receive distinct impressions from the spirit world; you feel so sure of your guide, and that everything is going to be alright.

The denseness and heaviness which you experience is because you are literally in a psychic fog, which the spiritual sunlight cannot penetrate. At such times cling with all your strength to the consciousness that the sun *is* there, that your helpers are still closely with you. This has a great bearing on your psychic and spiritual development, because so much depends on your poise, the quality of your character. You must train yourself to become a reflector not of confusion, but a steady and reliable reflector of spiritual reality.

There are times to work, times to rest. It is good to know how and when to relax, and to discriminate between on the one hand ease and relaxation, and on the other a collapse of courage and hope. People can and do go to pieces; they lose their poise, and say many things they do not mean. While you must be easy and relax, your spirit must always be in command. Do not let it be driven out by fear or prostration, for this means the captain of the ship has gone.

Make this pledge with your higher self, 'I will remain captain of my ship'; for to do this is to follow the true path of spiritual development.

Meditate often on the presence of your Master. You cannot even think of that radiant personality without some change taking place in your soul-body. When you meditate on him your whole being participates in his radiance.

7

Those who would bring peace into the lives of others, who would soothe the troubled breast or with a word of wisdom 'cast out devils', must first learn to control their own being.

Jesus knew that he could not command the forces of the unseen until he had complete command of the forces within himself. And those who would penetrate the mysteries of the universe, and understand the complexities of human relationships, rather than seek to put this and that person right, must first look within, they must set their own house in order.

You have been taught that if you hold the right thought, you become a focal point for the forces of good to work in your life. But more than this, you will find understanding of all the mysteries by following the simple teachings of the Master. If you submit yourself in love to God, He will work through you and you cannot go wrong. Love cannot err; love knows no evil; love knows no injustice; love is neither weak nor proud; love gives—and love withholds.

Those who would develop the gift of clair-voyance should seek the inner sanctuary of their own being. Attune yourselves to the celestial mind, and what will be revealed will not be a figment of imagination—it will be truth. Psychic gifts are useful, but remember that they only operate on the planes immediately surrounding the earth. Spiritual powers have no limit. With psychic powers you depend on certain conditions of the human body, of the human life, but with the development of spiritual gifts your power to penetrate the unseen realms becomes unlimited. Each one of you has latent spiritual powers, and as you seek to drink of the divine waters, those spiritual gifts will unfold as the lily to the sun.

You will often hear of the symbol of the water lily being used in spiritual unfoldment. The lily shown on the surface of the water is an ancient symbol of the unfolding spiritual gifts. If you would cultivate gifts of the spirit, first close your eyes and ears to all that is physical, then create a vision, or a mental picture, of a harmonious, beautiful garden. Walk through your garden to the innermost sanctuary, passing through the wide-open gate; and within that inner garden, see the silent pool, pure and still and so clear . . . still water of the spirit is clear as crystal. You may look into that water, and see the true reflection of yourself, for the waters of the spirit never lie. On the surface of the water you will see the lily, pure white, with a centre of gold—white and gold, symbolical of purity and divine intelligence. Rest quietly in contemplation of this perfect flower.

.   .   .

Behold now a cloud of unseen witnesses are with you. See the radiant forms around you, see the forms of the angels, and personal loved ones draw close and become at one with you. Behold there is no separation in God's universe. You are in God, and God is in you. Your guide is in you, is part of you, and you are part of your guide, there is no separation. All are of God, and there is no separation in God. You are in God, and God is perfect.

Come, children, to the waters of the living spirit; let all material adversity fall from you, and know only one truth—you are in God, and He makes all things plain!

God bless you all!

IV

Seek first the Kingdom

You all have your own particular difficulties and sorrows, your own particular fears. We cannot take these away from you, but we can help you to help yourselves; we can help you to rise above the darkness and heaviness of life in the outer world.

Each one of you is striving to reach your goal of the soul perfected, which will bring love and joy into your heart, and which will bring you health.

You find it difficult to believe that the sickness, loneliness or tribulation you suffer is the result of your own soul's wish. But it is so. Never blame other people for your troubles. Always look within and seek the divine love within your heart; then the reason for the conditions which limit you will become clear, and you will see the work you have to do *within yourself*. Man can only rise by making the effort to put aside all that troubles him, and reach up to the heaven world.

If you are separated from one you love, remember that love lives beyond the physical life and that you can meet your beloved in meditation. You cannot be separated unless you yourself draw down the shutters. Rise in thought and prayer to that spiritual state free from earthly ties, and at that level find perfect communion and happiness.

Be of good courage, and never forget your guardian angel and guide who are ever near, helping you to reach the state of peace and communion. You make your guide so happy when you make the effort to rise in spirit.

Do not be afraid. Nothing can hurt you if you resign yourself to the love of God.

It is foolish to fret; your problems always come right in the end; so why not walk hand in hand with your guide, knowing that all is working out according to God's plan; and that even in the midst of the hardest karma, God's mercy and love may be traced. Trust in God's love.

2

In the realms of spirit there is no limitation of time or space. When you think of the solar system or of the brethren on Venus or any other planet, you think in terms of distance;

you think of them as being far away, but this is not so. They are more evolved than men on earth at the present time and are not limited by distance.

On the other hand, if you think of a friend who, in earthly terms of measurement, is far away, you do not make a tedious journey in order to meet him. You are just with him, close to him. In the disembodied life this is actually what we do. We think in terms of love and we are with the beloved.

The soul who worships and truly loves God and the Christ is *instantly* at the heart of the great life and light. Circumstances may seem arduous to you while you are on earth. As you journey onward difficulties confront you and they have to be overcome; but truly there are no difficulties in the way of the spirit, because the spirit is *en rapport* with the whole of divine life, and in divine life or love there is no separation, no difficulty. This may sound complex to you, but try to realise it. When you do so, you will touch the plane of the Masters. The Master-thought comes to humanity on impulses or waves of love, and whenever the human soul touches or is touched by, or is in tune with that spiritual impulse, it sees quite clearly how matter can be mastered.

By your aspiration to God, by your impulse to do good, you open yourselves to a universe of incalculable power. As soon as you attune your instrument to the tuning note you are *there*, and They are with you. The Master-mind, the Master-spirit is using you.

3

God's plan is perfect. Why then do you allow yourself to become so anxious and worried? Nothing happens by chance; all is ordered by divine law. When man sins or breaks spiritual law, the result of his foolishness is always put to good use by divine law. Thus God is always repairing, always healing the nations, always healing souls, and though it may seem to you certain things happen by chance, in fact every-thing works together according to the divine will. Always remember this, and having done your best with the material at hand, surrender the rest to the divine love and perfect law. Have no fear or anxiety but surrender your life and affairs into the hands of the Great White Spirit.

Seek first the kingdom of heaven; seek the communion table and be strengthened in your heart for whatever lies before you. If you trust in God, without fail His love will flow through all your affairs, and you will know peace of heart.

God is all love and all wisdom. All He asks of His children is love; that they express love in all their ways.

4

You all have to learn the lesson of patience and tranquillity.

You think this means just waiting and waiting endlessly. I can hear some of you thinking, 'But we *are* patient, White Eagle. We *have* been waiting patiently.' The whole of life, my brother, my sister, has to be lived in patience, because right up to the very time of your release from the body you will be learning this lesson. To be patient really means to have confidence in God, knowing deep within your heart that God has you in His care and is working out a wise and beautiful purpose in your soul.

Do not feel that you must get over the ground as quickly as possible to reach a certain point. Just live every moment, every hour, every day, tranquilly in the protective love of God, taking the hours as they come and doing one thing at a time.

As soon as you start to think in terms of

getting somewhere or doing something as soon as possible, you lose your contact. Keep your vision on the Star, brethren, and live tranquilly in God, in God's time. Every morning when you awaken and every night before you sleep, just send out a thought to the Great White Spirit. That is all. Just feel that He is in your heart and that you are a son-daughter of that living power.

Whatever your need, God knows it. God is divine wisdom and intelligence as well as love; God is divine justice, and all things work together for good. When you realise this, you find peace. If your motive is good, you are good. God is caring for you and at the right time whatever you hope for will come. On earth you see all the difficulties and problems and you judge your fellows, you judge life because it is not to your liking. But when you realise that all that you can see has a purpose and is helping humanity to evolve, to develop understanding, to develop consciousness of God, then you will know that all is well.

5

'May the rose bloom upon your cross.' Interpreted this means, may you, through constant striving towards the Light, transmute the heaviness of the cross of matter into the fragrant rose of the spiritual life. On earth all you want has to be earned or worked for. In the same way all true joy and attainment comes only through effort, through the growth, the development of your spirit. So may you not grow weary in your effort. Keep on keeping on your path, and when times are difficult pray for the vision of the Star of Christ, create the vision of the Star, and never forget those who are guiding you individually and the world as a whole to the manifestation of the light of the Christ on earth.

Some people think that to be peaceful and to endeavour to pour oil on troubled waters is a sign of weakness; but let us use the word 'meekness' rather than 'weakness'. The Lord Christ is meek, but he is all-power; and peace is a dynamic power in the individual and in the nation. The peaceful spirit is powerful for good. Bring this spirit through matter; use matter, do not let matter, your lower self, drive out this peace, this power, this divine life, this happiness. Never doubt the goodness, the wisdom of God.

Nothing is more important than your soul's knowledge and love of God. Nothing is more important than that you walk steadfastly on the path of light. The first and greatest claim on you is the claim of God, or of your spirit, or, in other words, your highest self. Your true self is a shining spirit, a drop in the ocean of eternal life. You must above all be true, to that shining spirit.

You are serving your brethren in the true way by following the Light and obeying the dictates of your highest self. Do not allow yourself to be drawn into the darkness of earthly conflict; learn to rise above conflict and become strongly attached to the eternal verities. There you will find truth and love and happiness; there you will find freedom, and there you will be able to give the greatest help to your brethren and to all humanity.

6

Every one of you at some time, perhaps all the time, longs for peace. You think of peace as meaning goodwill towards each other, goodwill among the nations, the laying down of arms. But peace is far more than this; it can only be understood and realised within your heart. It lies beneath all the turmoil and noise and clamour of the world, beneath feeling, beneath thought. It is found in the deep, deep silence and stillness of the soul. It is spirit: in other words, it is God, your Creator.

How can man find this peace? It is not found by thinking about it, by using mental powers to comprehend it. No, my children, the Star will guide you to it, the Star which shone and still shines over the stable at Bethlehem. Think of the stable with the divine Mother and Joseph, her protector. The divine Mother is Love, the life-giver, and Joseph, her protector, the good mind which thinks aright, watching over and protecting the Mother who gives birth to the Christ-child.

The Star draws all wise men and women to this holy mystery of the birth of the Christ in the heart. It is Love, which draws all creatures to it, animal and human and angelic; for even the angels worship at the birth-place of Christ, Who alone brings peace and goodwill to earth. Immediately you think of Christ, the Golden One, and allow His spirit to take possession of you, whatever your emotional disturbance, grief or anxiety, the Christ spirit that is born in your heart brings you peace—peace which neither the mind nor the world can give or take away.

Now, will you hold in your inner vision the picture of a soft pink rose, symbol of divine

Mother love? As you create the form, inhale the fragrance of the rose, feel the softness of the petals, and looking into the centre see there the sparkling jewel of the Christ spirit. This should release in you a beautiful spiritual power. . . .

All form is created by thought, by mind. We would have you remember that it is within the power of God's Son to create form by thought. The power is in you, in all people. Sometimes the thought-form is the result of careless or negative thoughts which create form which has little use. But God-thought, the right thought, creates the perfect form. When you worship, when you think of divine love, you create a most beautiful form, according to the sincerity of your worship.

We have created the image of the rose for you, and we want you to realise that this is a symbol of your own heart centre. To create this rose you have to think beautiful thoughts, to think softly, gently, radiantly—then the form of the rose comes on the etheric plane (because you are using etheric matter, which is so much more easily moulded by thought). When you on earth can create this perfect and beautiful flower you are making a resting place or a 'cave' for the birth of Christ; for in that heart centre, in that flower which your higher mind has created, the perfect jewel, the flashing jewel of spirit rests.

When you evolve spiritually you will find that naturally, spontaneously you will always be creating beautiful form in the ethers, and in the higher worlds. By your good thought you will spontaneously create good form, positive form, and in that form will be the cradle, the womb, the birth-place of the Christ-Son.

We have given you a very simple picture to convey a profound mystical truth.

V

Be Still

The world of spirit is all around and within you. Within you is the power of God, and as you continually affirm in your heart that God dwells in you, that you are living in God, so the power of God will guide you. Whatever your need, forget physical things and concentrate wholly on the eternal spirit deep within you. Always, without equivocation, obey the light within you. Obey the voice of your spirit, which is also the voice of your Master.

People run hither and thither to contact the Master. They think that if they can breathe the same atmosphere as the Master they will be getting near to heaven; but this is not the way. Every soul will meet the Master in due time, but the Master is so close to you that you do not recognise him. The Master you have to serve and obey is right in your own heart. In time you will expand your consciousness until, at last, you will know the Master and recognise him. He will be in you, working through you, commanding every atom of your body and your soul.

Strive humbly and with love, to meet the Master in your own inner world, to know him in your heart, so that you may eventually be used by the Light to guide and help your younger brethren.

2

We would not have you think of the Master Jesus as a remote figure on a throne far removed from you and your daily life, for if you do so you are erecting a barrier between you and him. The Master Jesus is a strong, spiritually powerful soul, but he is also very human. He is very gentle, but noble in appearance; his face is bearded, his forehead beautifully formed, his features perfect. A striking feature of the Master Jesus is the beauty of his hands and feet.

Jesus has a powerful link with the present age. He is in a sense preparing the soul of humanity for the next outpouring of the Christ Light. He is at the head of the healing ray, and together with the work of healing bodies is the work of healing souls. He brings wisdom and love to the souls of men and women. He is concerned with philosophy and healing; for all true healing is linked with knowledge of spiritual things and also with the psychic forces in this world and beyond the world. If you are a healer you can be sure that you will receive the help of the Master Jesus. He is of course also working with the Brotherhood because the work of the Brotherhood is to heal the soul of mankind. When you project the light of the Star you are pouring forth healing power into the world, into the souls of men and women.

Jesus radiates compassion and love. He has borne, and bears still, a very heavy burden. He made the greatest sacrifice by surrendering himself utterly and completely to the Christ spirit. He surrendered his physical body to the use of the Christ. He gave all, and he brings that spirit of surrender and sacrifice to all who would work with him. He helps you to feel a tender love for all mankind. He stimulates within you that spirit which brings an inflow of love and happiness. When you surrender your way and your will to God, you immediately feel peace and an indescribable happiness.

Think of Jesus as being most human, gay, happy, understanding, and full of love.

3

Your thoughts of love never fail to reach those you love who have passed onward. When the body dies, the angels of death, who are God's messengers, take the sleeping soul and bear it tenderly through the mists surrounding the earth, and place it on a couch in its new home. All earthly fear is left behind.

You people on earth fear death very much. Yet in reality it is not *you* who fear death. It is really only the body that fears it. Death is the angel sent to draw the unwilling bolt and set the spirit free.

If man would live in close communion with those whom he loves in the heaven world, he must create through aspiration the conditions on the earth for the heavenly beings to come to him. You cannot imagine the angels being able to reach humanity in vibrations that are harsh and inharmonious, or where there is broken rhythm: but where there is harmony they can draw very close.

Spirit is fed by spirit. Your spirit, enclosed in your physical body, is fed from the heavenly world. *You* must make the effort to cut yourself away from the harshness, the broken rhythm, and the disharmony of a very material world, and tune your instrument to the higher wave-length, to the harmony of the spheres of heaven.

All disability, sickness and anxiety is the result of what we would describe as broken rhythm, or broken contact with the Source of life, with the Creator. To be healed you must forget material things, and tune-in to the spiritual life; you must seek freedom through communion with Christ and the Christ circle.

God knows your need. He knows the need of your soul, as well as your body. The soul comes first. And when the soul is made whole, the physical body leaps for joy.

4

In your daily life you can, if you so will, attain tranquillity of mind instantly. By an effort of the Will of God within you, you can still the storm, you can become tranquil and serene.

You long to become aware of a life which is free, holy, happy, and joyous; you long to see into the Land of Light, the promised land which Moses saw. *You can see it*. We point the way for you.

Let nothing disturb the tranquillity of your spirit. Immediately you allow things to disturb you, all the fine threads of colour which are attached to your soul from the Source of your life, become tangled and jangled and criss-crossed; in very truth, you 'cross the wires' and then you wonder why things are so difficult. Do not cross the wires. Keep your line of contact untangled and smooth. Be tranquil and serene in spirit. All those who have seen into the promised land remain tranquil. One who is a master of his life is never perturbed.

Sometimes we see you are anxious because you are not doing the work you want to do; you feel that you are overcharged with power and you could do so much if only you were given the opportunity to do so. We would remind you that you may not always choose your path. You stand before your Master awaiting his orders. You are sometimes impatient; you demand and you expect instant action, instead of trusting your Heavenly Father and His ministers, trusting those who have you in their care.

Each morning before your day's work give yourselves to the Divine Presence; then your day will be peaceful and happy. You will be filled with power to accomplish the will of God.

Jesus said: Put the Kingdom of God first, and all things will be added unto you. Seek first this Kingdom. Seek first God. Do not worry about the things of the mind and the flesh which pull at you. Go straight for the mark, the Christ spirit, and having God, your life will be filled with happiness of which no man can rob you.

VI

Think, Speak and Act in the Light

Be resolute, brethren, be strong in the Christ spirit. Strive to overcome all egotism. Be not self-opinionated, but surrender your heart and mind in humility to the supreme love and wisdom of your Creator, the heavenly Father and the divine Mother.

Thought is the most powerful influence in your life. Life *is* thought, and as a man thinks, so he becomes. Therefore if you truly desire to help your fellow man, look to your thoughts. Be strong in the Lord; be true to the Christ spirit which is within you, and so be master of the lodge of your own beings.

You have to submit and accept your karma—this is true, but you can submit and accept with the spirit of Christ in you, and you can bless your so-called enemies and do good to those who use you despitefully. When this becomes part of your life and consciousness, you then enter into the ocean of divine peace and love and happiness and you can truly bless mankind. This is the work waiting for every brother. Brothers should be strong in the Lord Christ and help their younger brethren to be strong.

Good thought, God-thought will rule the world and this is what the Brotherhood is working for. For we know that good thought, God-thought, right thought, loving thought will be the salvation of the human race.

Live for God, brethren, overcome all egotism; keep the mind and body pure and healthy. Seek health—for this is vital—a healthy mind and body. So you must follow the path of pure living—eat pure food, breathe pure air, think pure thoughts. We speak with all love and understanding, with all sympathy for you in your difficulties, especially in your difficulties with the physical body. It can be a task-master, but, dear brethren, rise superior to the physical and earthly pull and then you will very soon find life becomes easier. Put your hand in the hand of God, and all will work together for good—for God—in your life.

If you think rightly, miracles will happen.

2

You wonder why we emphasise the beauty of life, and apparently ignore that which is inharmonious and unbeautiful. From your earthly point of view you may feel a little rebellious, thinking, 'O, why emphasise the *so* little beauty and ignore the overwhelming sorrow and ignorance and darkness?'

It is because we can see so much more than you of the transcendent beauty of the spiritual life, and of mortal life also. Even while we are speaking to you now we hear the song of the birds in the trees outside this building, as music to our souls. We feel the companionship of these flowers on the altar; we see the forms of the nature spirits who guard them, and are responsible for their beauty and fragrance. These little nature spirits are our companions, our brothers.

What a glorious world! Leaving the city, we can go into fields of wild flowers, see freshly shooting corn and trees laden with the promise of fruit. We see in the skies countless millions of nature spirits, all working together for the good of life, and to bring gifts of food and sustenance to humanity. We see all around you in this chapel the forms of radiant teachers and angelic beings, waiting to serve, to fill your souls with love and peace. We see that through the music you have heard, the angels of music are drawn close to serve you, touching your souls as hands play upon a harp, so that you also may absorb the harmony of the spheres of music.

Do you wonder, then, that we continually emphasise the gifts of God, poured forth so liberally upon you, His children? Do you not see, beloved brethren, that in the degree that you respond to love and beauty, so you are increasing beauty on earth; and by the same token decreasing that which lies on the other side of the scale—the darkness and ignorance and bitterness and selfishness of humanity?

We know the sordidness and ugliness in man's life, but it is our work and yours to dispel that sordidness. We move forward on a path leading us ever upward and onward towards the kingdom of heaven; and by every thought and act in our daily life we can create joy, happiness and love, and thus help forward God's great plan of evolution.

3

You say, 'White Eagle, you tell us to control our thoughts—but it is not possible!'

I will give you a simple exercise. When you have a piece of work to do, even if it is only hammering a nail into a piece of wood, do it with all your care. Concentrate your whole being on the job in hand. Do not do one thing while thinking about a dozen others. Make yourself interested in the particular piece of work in hand. How often do you listen to a conversation and absorb nothing? The conversation may seem to you to be futile—but perhaps *you* are the foolish one. Forget everything else but your companion as you are conversing with him. Concentrate your whole attention on what he is saying. Courtesy at least demands this. If the Master should come and you, not knowing it was he, talked to him—possibly foolishly—the Master would take notice of your every word. For the time being your conversation would be all that mattered to him. Take this very seriously, because it offers a practical and simple method of thought control. Centre your whole attention on what you are doing, always.

Don't go about with your eyes shut; be intelligent, interested and alive, and concentrate on the point of the moment. This is the first step towards thought control. Then you will begin to be of value to your Master and to your own guide, as an instrument of the Light.

Remember that the mind is the slayer of the real. Set aside destructive thought. Throw it out, and attune yourself to the one keynote of life—love.

Although it has its value, do not be carried away by earthly intellect; the mind is so powerful that you can safely allow the heart full play, and you cannot go wrong if you let your heart guide you always. The age of the mind is a dangerous age, and because of this the Wise Ones work constantly to bring about a blending of the mind and the heart. The mind is the destroyer, and the heart the preserver. The heart is, in a sense, the great Mother, the womb of life. Let your search be beneath the surface. Let your search be in the heart of humanity. Act from the heart. Do not be content with words; get to the inner meaning of life, to the heart of a brother, to the heart of a group, to the heart of humanity, and the heart of the earth.

The Rose of divine Love is the heart.

4

The power of thought is the creative power of all life, but in most human souls it remains quiescent. You must learn to use your God-thought. Within you all is this divine principle which has power to create vibration among, and to control, the actual atoms of matter.

We would teach you also that the simple word which is so much used, with so little understanding, the word *GOD*, has a tremendous power. The more you send forth the vibration of God, or good, from your thoughts and from your heart, the more you are bringing into active manifestation the power of God. Do you not see the great power which lies dormant within you? It is God's gift to you, His child.

Jesus struck one dominant note throughout all his ministry, and it was this—'The Father that dwelleth in me, He doeth the works.' Jesus made no claim for himself that he did not share with all those who love God. When man realises this truth of the Christ within, then at last he will stand forth as a true son or daughter of God, and will meet his brother man on a common platform of brotherhood and service.

Are you not created in the image of God? What a birthright is yours! To hold the gift of the spirit within you so that you may become perfect sons of God the Father, going about your ministry even as Christ!

And in the words of the Master we say, 'Feed my sheep'—in daily service and love.

5

We would leave you with a thought to meditate on during the coming days. Courage! As servants of the Christ you must never lack courage. You will be tempted to do so, for the shadows group around you and tempt you to be weary, to have no confidence; they tempt you to say, 'I am no use', and to have what you call 'an inferiority complex'. This is actually conceit, not humility.

If you are anxious and fearful, you draw about yourself a veil of self-pity, which is of no use to you because it is not constructive. You must be constructive, you must draw to yourself the power which the brethren in the Great White Lodge are continually concentrating upon you. It is for you to take.

You must have courage for your work; courage to heal, to comfort; courage to give service, and courage never to doubt God's power, or the power of God to work through you. To think you are no good is to doubt God's power. Of yourself you are merely a channel, but that which dwells in you, the power of God, is the directing, controlling, creative principle in life. God Who has created the universes, the myriad stars and the planets with their influence upon this earth; Who has set in motion the great cycles and those cosmic rays which play and interplay upon this earth plane to affect the individual life—that same divine principle will create through you.

6

The six-pointed Star under which you work is the symbol of the perfectly balanced life, the symbol of the Christ-man and the Christ in man. It is the great symbol of man made perfect and it forms the foundation of matter as well as the expression of spirit. We are thinking at the moment of the snowflake, and the many forms in the natural world which are based on the six points of the Star.

If you can think of yourself as being composed of countless millions of tiny six-pointed stars, you may begin to realise your power—no, not your own power, but the power of God within you. Man is restricted and limited and to a degree cowed, because, through long habit of thought and life, he has become bound in a low degree of consciousness. Yet within every man is this power of God which will develop as soon as he responds to his natural urge to love and to give. Through many lives man has neglected to respond to love. He has desired, not to give, but to take—to draw things to himself; and in this possessiveness he has lost the key to his own power-house.

But never forget that you have within yourself this power, this light, generated by love; and that you have to train yourself through love towards God and man, to generate this light, this dynamic power. The light of the spirit can shine from your heart, from your whole body. The heart-centre of man can be like a lighted torch on a dark night, and can cast a beam into darkened highways. This is the very light of the universe, the true light of God, the dynamic force which can perform miracles. There is nothing—no problem, no difficulty, no limitation which cannot be overcome by the accumulated power of millions of tiny stars within yourself; or the Star of Bethlehem, the Star of Christ shining in your heart.

The Star of Bethlehem is this Star of love, a Star of true peace—not a static peace, but dynamic and powerful.

Let us then conceive the blazing Star as a symbol of the dynamic force and true light which interpenetrates all matter, and know it as the key to the overcoming of ignorance, fear, unhappiness, and evil.

God created human beings to be happy, my brethren, not for a life of suffering. The Father–Mother God created earth children for happiness, and they will give *you* happiness; but you will have to open your heart and pass this happiness on to your brother.

7

Remember that God needs man through whom He can manifest.

Do all you can, not to preach, but to *live* the gospel, to shed light in darkness, to sow goodness where there is lack of goodness; through love and God-thought to stimulate the good in your brethren.

You can serve humanity in no better way than this, to be an instrument for the forces of the Light. Do not depend on this or that person for opportunities to serve; you have only to be your true self. You have only to surrender to God, to obey His will and accept His way and immediately you become a server; you are helping the world. There is no limit to the light which can pour through you and extend over the whole earth.

The world needs all the positive God-thought that you can project, to heal the sick in body and mind. In the silence of your own soul, kneel beside the still waters and pray to be able to send forth the healing light of the Son of God, the Christ. Behind you is a Power beyond your comprehension, waiting only for Its children to be channels. May the channel open wide and the light flood through you to heal the whole world and raise it from death and darkness into everlasting light and glory.

THE WHITE EAGLE PUBLISHING TRUST

NEW LANDS · LISS · HAMPSHIRE